Symbols of America

PRESIDENTIAL SEAL

TABLE OF CONTENTS

Presidential Seal 3

Glossary 22

Index 24

A Crabtree Seedlings Book

CRABTREE
Publishing Company
www.crabtreebooks.com

School-to-Home Support for Caregivers and Teachers

This book helps children grow by letting them practice reading. Here are a few guiding questions to help the reader with building his or her comprehension skills. Possible answers appear here in red.

Before Reading:

- What do I think this book is about?
    - *I think this book is about the seal of the President of the United States.*
    - *I think this book is about the reason why there is a presidential seal.*

- What do I want to learn about this topic?
    - *I want to learn more about the different characters on the presidential seal.*
    - *I want to learn more about inauguration parties.*

During Reading:

- I wonder why...
    - *I wonder why the presidential seal has a picture of a bald eagle on it.*
    - *I wonder why President Abraham Lincoln didn't use the presidential seal.*

- What have I learned so far?
    - *I have learned that the presidential seal is used when the president speaks at special events.*
    - *I have learned that the presidential seal is in the middle of the ceiling of the Oval Office.*

After Reading:

- What details did I learn about this topic?
    - *I have learned that President Rutherford B. Hayes was the first president to use a presidential seal.*
    - *I have learned that the presidential limousine and airplane use the seal.*

- Read the book again and look for the vocabulary words.
    - *I see the word **represents** on page 7, and the word **shield** on page 12. The other glossary words are on pages 22 and 23.*

PRESIDENTIAL SEAL

The **presidential** seal is a **symbol** of America.

It is the **official** symbol of the president of the United States.

It is based on the Great Seal of the United States.

There is a circle of 50 stars.

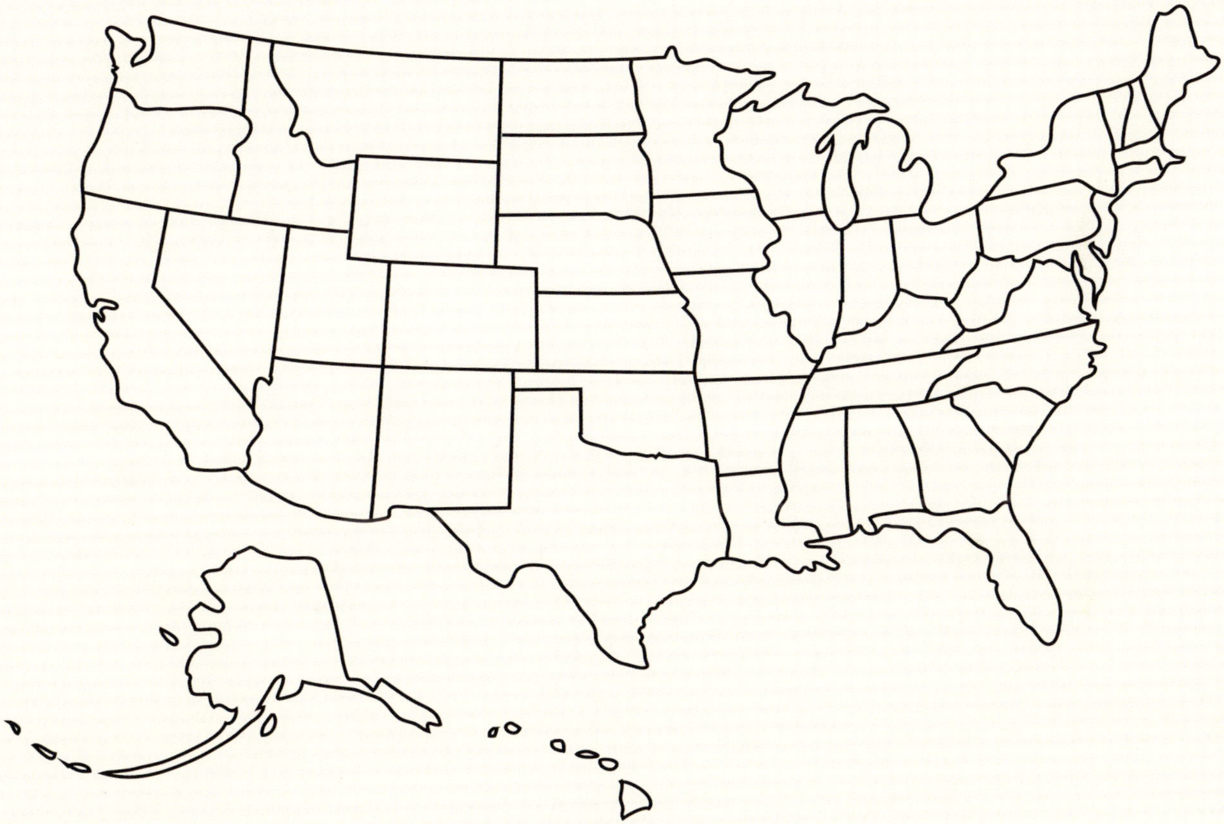

Each star **represents** a state.

The presidential seal has a bald eagle.

The eagle holds 13 arrows and a branch with 13 olives and leaves.

The eagle's beak holds a ribbon. The phrase on the ribbon means "Out of many, one."

The bald eagle is a symbol of the United States.

The **shield** has 6 red stripes and 7 white stripes.

There are 13 stars and 13 clouds.

President Rutherford B. Hayes was the first president to use a presidential seal. He used it on White House invitations.

President Abraham Lincoln used his own special seal.

The seal is used when the president speaks at special events.

The presidential limousine and airplane use the seal.

The presidential seal is used on coins, badges, china, and the rug in the Oval Office.

The seal is also in the middle of the ceiling of the Oval Office.

E PLURIBUS UNUM

New presidents dance over the seal at **inauguration** parties.

The presidential seal is an important symbol of America.

Glossary

inauguration (uh-naa-gyr-AY-shn): A ceremony that marks the beginning of something

official (uh-FI-shl): Relating to a decision by those in charge

presidential (preh-zuh-DEN-chl): Relating to a president

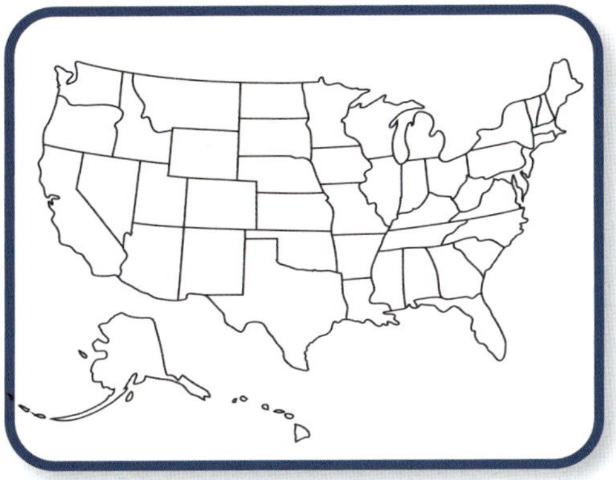

represents (reh-pruh-ZENTS): Symbolizes something officially

shield (sheeld): A piece of metal used for protection

symbol (SIM-bl): A thing that represents something else

Index

bald eagle 8, 10, 11

Hayes, Rutherford B. 14

inauguration 20

invitations 14

Oval Office 18

Lincoln, Abraham 15

About the Author

Christina Earley lives in sunny South Florida with her husband and son. She enjoys traveling around the United States and learning about different historical places. Her hobbies include hiking, yoga, and baking.

CRABTREE Publishing Company

Written by: Christina Earley

Designed by: Kathy Walsh

Proofreader: Petrice Custance

Photographs: Shutterstock: cover: ©DavidScar; ©MT511, ©dz; Title Pg: ©MT511, ©dz; Pg 4-21 ©MT511; Pg 3 21-23: ©nazlisart, Pg 3, 22, 23: ©Marian Weyo; Pg 4, 22 ©solomonjee: Pg 5: ©AlexanderZavadsky; Pg 6: © CarryLove; Pg 7 © Berkah Icon; Pg 9: ©Christos Georghiou; Pg 11: ©OpenRangeStock; Pg 13, 23: ©DavidScar; Pg 14: ©Everett Collection; Pg 15: @Wiki, ©Everett Collection; Pg 16: © Joseph Sohm; Pg 17: ©1000 Words; Pg 18: @Wiki; Pg 19: ©amadeustx; Pg 21: ©ungvar;.Pg 20, 22: @Wiki

Library and Archives Canada Cataloguing in Publication
CIP available at Library and Archives Canada

Library of Congress Cataloging-in-Publication Data
CIP available at Library of Congress

Crabtree Publishing Company
www.crabtreebooks.com 1-800-387-7650

Printed in the U.S.A./072022/CG20220201

Published in the United States
Crabtree Publishing
347 Fifth Avenue, Suite 1402-145
New York, NY, 10016

Published in Canada
Crabtree Publishing
616 Welland Ave.
St. Catharines, Ontario L2M 5V6